Savvy

Girls Rock

GIRLS RULE!

AMAZING TALES OF FEMALE LEADERS

BY SHELLEY TOUGAS

Consultant:
Julie Novkov
Professor of Political Science and
Women's Studies
University at Albany
State University of New York

Library of Congress Cataloging-in-Publication Data
Tougas, Shelley.
Girls rule! : amazing tales of female leaders / by Shelley Tougas.
    pages cm.—(Savvy. Girls rock!)
Includes bibliographical references and index.
Summary: "Through narrative stories, explores female leaders who have made major contributions in business, government, or other organizations"—Provided by publisher.
Audience: Grade 4 to 6.
ISBN 978-1-4765-0235-9 (library binding)—ISBN 978-1-4765-3565-4 (ebook pdf)
1. Women—Biography—Juvenile literature. 2. Women executives—Biography—Juvenile literature. 3. Leadership in women—Juvenile literature. I. Title.
CT3207.T68 2014
920.72—dc23
2013008191

Editorial Credits
Jennifer Besel, editor; Veronica Scott, designer; Wanda Winch, media researcher; Laura Manthe, production specialist

Photo Credits
AP Images: Carolyn Kaster, 35; Clara Barton National Historic Site, National Park Service, 53 (right); Collection of the Supreme Court of the United States/Steve Petteway, 38-39; Corbis: AP/Thibault Camus, 49 (middle), Bettmann, 10, Bob Krist, 36 (top), Douglas Kirkland, 51 (r), Louie Psihoyos, 56, Neville Elder, 49 (left), Nora Feller, 48, Peter Turnley 11, 20, Reuters, 23, Reuters/ berly White, 49 (r), SABA/Najlah Feanny, 33 (bottom), Sygma/Kapoor Baldev, 27, Sygma/Michel Philippot, 8, Xinhua Press, 52, Zuma Press/Martin Klimek, 4-5; Courtesy of the White House: Samantha Appleton, 47 (b); Dreamstime: Philcold, 28; Htoo Tay Zar, 9; John F. Kennedy Library and Museum: Abbie Rowe, 46; Library of Congress: Prints and Photographs Division, 15, 24 (br), 33 (t), 42 (b), 44, 47 (t), 50, 53 (l), 59 (t), Marion S. Trikoso, 31; Newscom: akg-images, 16, akg-images/British Library, 29 (b), Everett Collection, 57, Getty Images Inc/AFP/Stephane De Sakutin, 36 (b), PHOTOlink/ Lane Ericcson, 58, Picture History, 13, picture-alliance/dpa/John Macdougall, 41, SIPA/Dalmas, 37, SIPA/Picture Press Europe, 18, TELAM/ARCHIVO, 19, UPI/Alexis C. Glenn, 32, Zuma Press/Arthur Grace, 25 (tl), Zuma Press/Pittsburgh Post-Gazette, 55; Photo by Mathew Brady, image courtesy of J Godsey, 24 (tl); Shutterstock: anemad, 3, 62-64, Apostrophe, 6-7 (back), Atlaspix, 42 (t), Augusto Cabral, 45, donatas1205, 14, Featureflash, 61, Gizele, 51(l), ilolab, 36-37 (back), Kamira, 21, 26, Karakotsya, 17, Katya Ulitina, 50 (t), Kjpargeter, cover, 1 (all), Maria Timofeeva, 54-55 (back), McCarthy's PhotoWorks, 43 (Queen Elizabeth II, middle), Megin, 12, Michaelpuche, 43 (b), mistydawnphoto, 25 (tr), Neftali, 40-41 (back), Olga Besnard, 59 (m), Rafa Irusta, 28-29 (back), s_bukley, 59 (b), sellingpix, 42-43 (back), spirit of America, 34, Steve Mann, 43 (t), SWEvil, 30, Victoria Goncharenko, 10-11 (back); State Archives of Florida: Florida Memory, floridamemory.com/N041432, 14; SuperStock Inc/Pantheon, 29 (t); U.S. House of Representatives: Office of the Speaker, 25 (br); U.S. Senate Photographic Studio, 24 (tr); Walter P. Reuther Library/Wayne State University, 7; Wikipedia: Mrlopez2681, 43 (m)

Direct quotations are placed within quotation marks and appear on the following pages. Other pieces written in first-person point of view are works of creative nonfiction by the author.
p3: www.biography.com/people/eleanor-roosevelt-9463366; **p4:** www.cnn.com/2012/07/16/tech/web/marissa-mayer-bio/; **p6:** www.lasculturas.com/aa/bio/bioDoloresHuerta.htm; **p8:** www.cbc.ca/news/background/pakistan/bhutto-quotes.html; www.telegraph.co.uk/news/worldnews/1573795/Benazir-Bhutto-killing-Reaction-in-quotes.html; **p9:** www.journalgazette. net/article/20120923/LOCAL08/309239935/1044/LOCAL08; **p10:** www.brainyquote.com/quotes/authors/e/eleanor_ roosevelt.htm **p26:** news.bbc.co.uk/onthisday/hi/dates/stories/october/31/newsid_2464000/2464423.stm; thinkexist.com/ quotes/indira_gandhi/2.html; **p33:** www.mcslibrary.org/program/library/declaration.htm; **p35:** articles.cnn.com/2007-01- 20/politics/clinton.announcement_1_first-presidential-spouse-exploratory-committee-senate-bid?_s=PM:POLITICS; www. npr.org/templates/story/story.php?storyId=122152265; **p45:** www.brainyquote.com/quotes/authors/g/golda_meir_2.html; **p47:** www.biography.com/people/michelle-obama-307592; **p50:** www.biography.com/people/madam-cj-walker-9522174; **p52:** www.telegraph.co.uk/health/swine-flu/5251989/Profile-Dr-Margaret-Chan-leading-the-worlds-response-to-swine-flu. html; **p57:** www.brainyquote.com/quotes/authors/k/katie_couric_2.html#zLGJ4DGzbt0Zo8Bl.99

Printed in the United States of America in Stevens Point, Wisconsin.
032013   007227WZF13

GIRLS RULE

The world's most incredible women know there's a big difference between talking and doing. Leadership begins when ideas and action cross paths. Society changes when passionate leaders inspire and motivate others.

Women have earned top spots in business, science, art, media, and government. But it hasn't been easy.

WHERE THERE WAS WRONG, THEY STRIVED TO MAKE RIGHT.

WHERE THERE WAS DOUBT, THEY BELIEVED.

WHERE THERE WERE BARRIERS, THEY PERSISTED.

THEY LED WHEN IT WOULD HAVE BEEN EASIER TO FOLLOW.

"It is better to light a candle than curse the darkness."

– Eleanor Roosevelt

MARISSA MAYER

MAY 30, 1975–

Today the Internet is a part of most people's daily lives. But it wasn't always that way. It was Marissa Mayer who played a huge role in making the Internet what it is now.

Mayer earned an unusual college degree in the late 1990s. She studied artificial intelligence, which makes computers learn like a human brain. After college she took a job with a start-up company. She became the company's first female engineer.

With Mayer's help, this company revolutionized the Internet. What company was it?

GOOGLE

At Google Mayer earned a reputation for taking the fiction out of science fiction. She and her team improved searches and created Gmail. Mayer led the team that created Google Maps. Mayer's work can even be seen on Google's iconic homepage. She insisted on a simple design, with just the company's name and a small text box.

In 2012 Mayer shocked the technology world again. She left Google to take charge of Yahoo. She continues to do what no one thought a woman could.

"You can be good at technology and like fashion and art. You can be good at technology and be a jock. You can be good at technology and be a mom. You can do it your way, on your terms."

Dolores Huerta

APRIL 10, 1930–

DOLORES HUERTA LOOKED AROUND HER CLASSROOM IN CALIFORNIA'S FARM COUNTRY.

She looked past the books, backpacks, and pencils. She saw kids who were too hungry to learn. Their clothes either squeezed them tight or hung too loose. Everywhere she saw dirty hands and hungry stomachs. Instantly, she realized she'd picked the wrong job.

"I thought I could do more by organizing farmworkers than by trying to teach their hungry children."

These children's parents were mostly Mexican immigrants who worked as farm laborers. Farmworkers in the United States in the 1960s had few rights. Landowners required them to work long hours for little pay. If workers complained, their bosses fired them and hired someone else.

Huerta met with farmworkers and urged them to work together.

She showed them how to use group power to improve their lives. One person couldn't change working conditions. But together they had power to fight for change.

Huerta took their case to California lawmakers. Soon they passed new laws supporting immigrants, such as allowing voters to vote in Spanish.

When her group, United Farm Workers, organized a strike in 1965 for grape farmworkers, she became one of the nation's foremost union leaders. Over the next few years, she led boycotts and negotiated contracts. She won public assistance for workers, fought for services for farmers' children, and more.

Her legacy is bigger than the battles she won. Those laborers felt powerless and didn't believe they could change a system run by the rich. Huerta proved they could change their lives, but only if they united and fought as a group.

BENAZIR BHUTTO

JUNE 21, 1953–DECEMBER 27, 2007

My father commanded the fight for democracy in Pakistan. He championed the people's voice throughout his entire government career. The people believed in him, and they elected him prime minister in Pakistan's first democratic election. Then in 1977 the military arrested my father, took over the country, and then killed him.

"I told him on my oath in his death cell, I would carry on his work."

I began traveling the country. I rallied crowds, demanding free elections and basic rights. Timing was on my side. The military leader died, and I ran in Pakistan's first election since the soldiers took control, and I won.

I was the first female prime minister in an Islamic country. At only 35, I'd fulfilled my promise to my father.

Leading Pakistan was difficult. Most men didn't trust me. They blocked my ideas for civil rights, education, and ending poverty.

My family paid a heavy price for our leadership. Not only was Father killed, my brother mysteriously died. My opponents accused me of corruption and removed me from office. Police arrested my mother and me. I was imprisoned, and later I was forced to leave my own country.

Finally I returned to continue the fight. I ran again for office and survived one assassination attempt. But the second attempt succeeded. My killers were never brought to justice.

My friend wrote, "She knew the risks but was determined to stay."

AUNG SAN SUU KYI

JUNE 19, 1945–

In a tiny country run by the military, Aung San Suu Kyi has been a soldier for democracy. She's never picked up a weapon. She's fought with brains, courage, and determination. All she asks is for free elections in the Asian nation known as Burma.

"Government leaders are amazing. So often it seems they are the last to know what the people want."

In 1988 Suu Kyi returned to Burma after going to school in Great Britain. In Burma she found the military government violently punishing anyone who spoke against it. She began giving speeches and writing public letters opposing the government. The government quickly put Suu Kyi under house arrest, cutting her off from any communication with the outside world.

Suu Kyi was released from house arrest a few times. But each time she went right back to protesting and building the National League for Democracy party. Again and again, she was arrested. Suu Kyi spent a total of 15 years under house arrest.

Although she was cut off from the world, the world noticed her. International leaders have honored Suu Kyi with nearly 50 humanitarian awards, including the Nobel Peace Prize.

In 2012, under international pressure, rulers allowed her to run for office. Suu Kyi won a seat in the governing body. She will continue to serve in her country, but only if that's what the people want.

I scrambled from the boat onto the rocky shore of Alcatraz. My sister and I walked the steep path to the former prison. The scene stunned us.

A protester's message covered a cement wall. "You are on Indian Land."

I no longer saw a prison. As an American Indian, I saw freedom and justice.

The protesters greeted us with hugs and smiles. A small group of American Indians had taken over this rock in San Francisco Bay to spotlight the injustices faced by our people. We were second-class citizens with bad schools, poor health care, and few jobs.

Within moments of arriving at Alcatraz, my sister and I decided to join the cause.

Alcatraz changed my life. I could no longer be a housewife and watch the news with indifference. I had to fight for equal rights and my heritage as a member of the Cherokee Nation.

I traveled between Alcatraz and our command post, talking to the media and lawmakers about the protest. The government ended the occupation, but I continued the fight. In 1985 tribal leaders selected me to be the first woman to lead the Cherokee Nation. We raised nearly $150 million a year, which we invested in schools and health care for all American Indians.

The success story lifted the hearts of my people. I gave many interviews to reporters and spoke at large conferences. Nationally, I became the face of the American Indian rights movement.

But for my people, I hope my face symbolized the promise of a better world.

AMERICAN INDIANS PROTESTING AT ALCATRAZ IN 1964

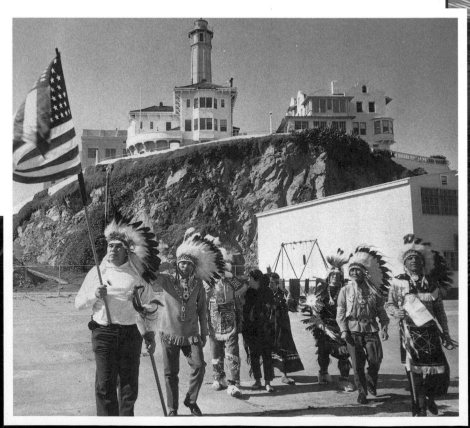

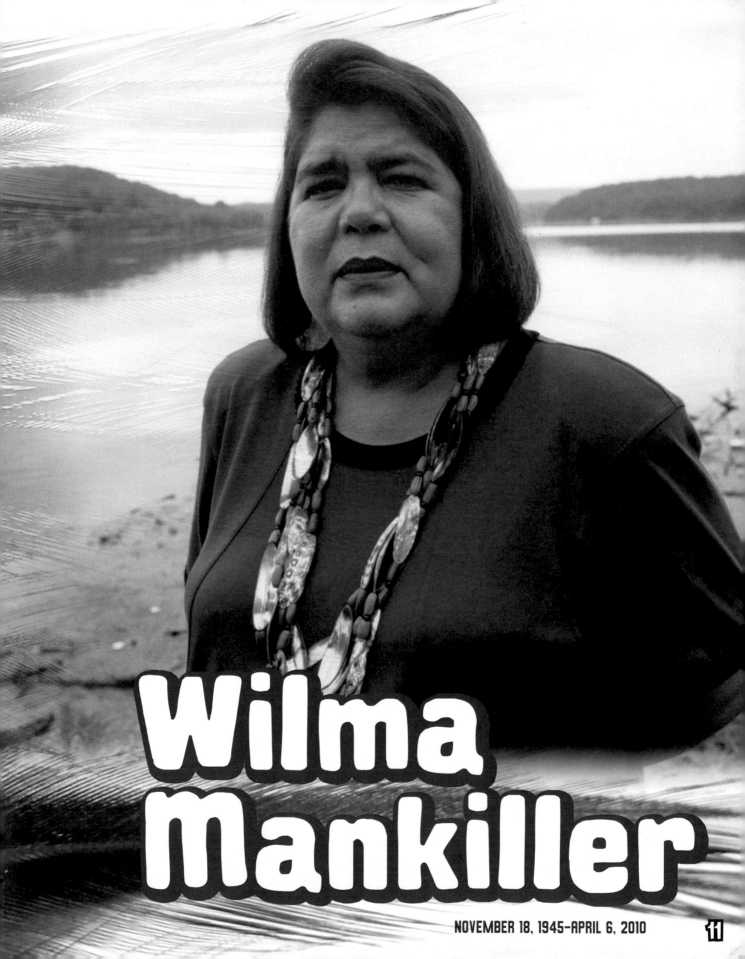

Wilma Mankiller

NOVEMBER 18, 1945–APRIL 6, 2010

Eleanor Roosevelt

As a wealthy young woman, Anna "Eleanor" Roosevelt was quiet and gentle. She lived a comfortable life in the early 1900s. But then Roosevelt saw the world outside her own—a world of poverty and citizens without basic rights.

AND ROOSEVELT ROARED.

Roosevelt urged the nation's women to stand against bad businesses and bad government. Writers called her "Everywhere Eleanor" because of her extensive travels and attention to multiple causes. She fought to end child labor and poverty. She fought for the rights of women, immigrants, and African-Americans. If Roosevelt saw injustice, she fought.

"A woman is like a tea bag. You never know how strong she is until she gets in hot water."

Her importance as a political activist surged when her husband, Franklin Roosevelt, was elected president. Most first ladies socialized with political wives and kept quiet. But Roosevelt jumped on the presidential stage as a partner. She advised her husband on major issues and used her popularity to call attention to her causes.

Roosevelt was one of the most politically active first ladies in modern history. She became a role model for women seeking a political voice and a hero for generations of activists, female and male.

MARY MCLEOD BETHUNE

JULY 10, 1875–MAY 18, 1955

Darkness swallowed everything in Bethune's vision. She stood alone in front of the school she had built.

The Ku Klux Klan, a secret organization that harassed, harmed, and even killed African-Americans, had promised to burn down Bethune's school that night. She prayed and wondered how she'd fight the Klan by herself.

The Klan didn't come that night, and she never found out why. But the fear she felt was a constant reminder that many white people didn't want black people to get an education.

Bethune's school for children was humble. She scrounged for supplies and was constantly trying to raise funds. But her hard work paid off. Eventually, the school included a farm, a high school, a nursing program, and a college.

Her work as an educator and organizer dazzled Washington, D.C. Soon she was advising presidents. To ensure African-American women had a voice in government, Bethune launched the National Council of Negro Women in 1935.

Bethune showed her community and country that education was key to escaping poverty. She proved that African-Americans could fight for social change.

She lived the lessons she taught.

BETHUNE WITH SEVERAL OF HER STUDENTS IN 1905

JANE ADDAMS

SEPTEMBER 6, 1860–MAY 21, 1935

People called Jane Addams unrealistic and childish. But she didn't care. She continued to talk and write and rally. She wanted peace above all else, and she wasn't going to stop working for it. She believed conflict could be settled without violence. She insisted that leaders could prevent war if they embraced peace as their goal.

But leaders called her a radical, an unrealistic person who wanted to rebuild society.

Addams was born in Cedarville, Illinois. Her father was a wealthy state senator who had important friends, including President Abraham Lincoln. Addams wanted for nothing during her childhood. As an adult, she became passionate about helping those less fortunate. She also developed a deep belief that peace was always the answer.

When war exploded in Europe in 1914, Addams had already gained recognition as an activist. She urged the United States to stay out of the war. But in 1917 the United States joined what would become World War I. Addams shamed war supporters.

People accused her of being unpatriotic. Newspapers wrote scathing articles about her. The Daughters of the American Revolution, a group that celebrates America's revolutionary founding, kicked her out.

But Addams pressed forward, taking leadership positions in the Women's Peace Party and the International Congress of Women. Addams proved women could make waves with passion, intelligence, and dedication.

In 1931 Addams' advocacy won recognition instead of criticism. The Nobel Prize committee honored her as the first woman to win the Nobel Peace Prize. It was a great honor for someone who just wanted to bring peace to the world.

Rosa Luxemburg

MARCH 5, 1871–JANUARY 15, 1919

It was the late 1800s. Rosa Luxemburg challenged Poland's leaders by giving speeches that claimed workers, not owners, should grab control of politics and money. Luxemburg urged workers worldwide to quit working until the government met their demands.

Many citizens liked what Luxemburg was saying. They wanted wealth shared more equally. But the government didn't like it at all.

Luxemburg escaped arrest by fleeing to Switzerland, then eventually to Germany. When she protested Germany's involvement in World War I, she ended up in prison for most of the war.

Her passion for a complete revolution grew in prison. After being released, she stepped up efforts to organize workers into a powerful political group. The German government wouldn't tolerate her protests. Luxemburg had become too loud, too passionate, and too admired. A secret arm of the government ordered her murder in 1919. They stopped her life but not her voice. Her speeches, books, and articles continue to spark debate among generations of activists.

QUEEN RANIA OF JORDAN

Rania al Yassin strolled into a dinner party after work. At the party she met Prince Abdullah II bin al-Hussein, heir to the throne of Jordan. The two quickly fell in love. Six months later they married.

Rania soared from a marketing job to the world stage. She had been born into an average family without political ties. But her personality, beauty, and intelligence captivated the media. Jordanians loved her.

Rania became queen in 1999, but she wasted no time relaxing on a throne. She created the Jordan River Foundation to empower women in a country that restricted their rights. Rania advocates for children, education, and health care. Her leadership has inspired millions of Muslim women to consider themselves activists and leaders.

Rania travels the world, wears western fashions, and socializes with the world's wealthiest people. She projects sincerity and love. Her citizens look beyond her title of queen. They cherish the woman who used to be one of them and still is at heart.

Workers in Argentina's Department of Labor and Welfare froze when the door opened. Eva Perón, wife of the president, marched into the office and announced her intention to work there.

And work she did. She worked directly with Argentina's poorest people—families in poverty seeking help. For Perón it wasn't a show. She genuinely cared and understood what the people were going through. For she had grown up in poverty too.

Perón showered charities with money and opened schools. She personally delivered food and clothes to the poor.

She added women's rights to her agenda. The former actress gave political speeches and even considered running as her husband's vice president. Perón's behavior alarmed Argentina's wealthy population. Government officials worried about her influence.

But Perón's work was stopped in its tracks. Cancer raged through her body. And at the age of 32, Eva Perón died.

Although she died young, her "power to the people" legacy spread across South America. Wives of leaders took note, and many followed her lead and used their positions for good.

Eva Perón

MAY 7, 1919–JULY 26, 1952

Winnie Mandela threatened to bring South Africa to its knees.

Tough, passionate, and fearless, Mandela waged war against apartheid, a system of governing that separates people based on race. Whites were the minority, but they controlled everything. Black South Africans lived in poverty and had few rights.

Mandela's activist husband, Nelson Mandela, was imprisoned in 1964. She took over the anti-apartheid cause. She defied the government, rallied crowds of black South Africans, and hinted that violence could be a tactic.

She risked her freedom and her life for her beliefs. Her campaign motivated others to never back down and to march to victory.

But Mandela's behavior grew more radical. Her speeches clearly promoted violence. Her bodyguards behaved like bullies and tortured black people they suspected of cooperating with white police. Some of her followers worried she'd become a danger to the cause.

In 1988 a 14-year-old black boy was murdered in Soweto, South Africa. Authorities accused Mandela and her bodyguards of the boy's kidnapping and death. They said Mandela suspected he had helped white police. Courts convicted Mandela of the crime. Her six-year prison sentence was reduced to a fine.

The government began to dismantle apartheid in 1990. Mandela's legacy divides the nation. Hero? Radical? The debate continues. But it's clear she was a powerful leader who kept the fight against apartheid alive.

WINNIE MANDELA

SEPTEMBER 26, 1936–

World leaders shook their heads in disbelief. Filipinos had elected a homemaker as president. Frankly, Corazon Aquino was not qualified to be president.

I should know. I am her only son.

My father fought for democracy while Mother stood by his side. A mother and a wife, she was not a politician or speechmaker. When Dictator Ferdinand Marcos ordered my father's murder, Father's supporters pressed Mother to fill his role.

She reluctantly agreed. Her timid first steps turned into a sprint. She led protests, calling Marcos a coward for not facing the ballot box. Mother became the face of reform. Pressure from Filipinos and other countries pushed Marcos into exile.

The election stunned the world. My mother became the first female president—not just in the Philippines but all of Asia! South Korea, Romania, Taiwan, and others soon adopted Mother's "People Power," her nonviolent way of changing government.

My sisters and I were proud. Mother lived my father's dream of democratic elections. *Time* magazine named her "Woman of the Year."

Mother left office peacefully in 1992. Why? She had passed a six-year limit on the presidency, a reform to ensure presidents wouldn't lust for power or lose touch with citizens. "People Power" wasn't a slogan for Mother. It is her legacy.

Corazon Aquino

JANUARY 25, 1933–AUGUST 1, 2009

FAMOUS FIRSTS

Victoria Woodhull

SEPTEMBER 23, 1838–JUNE 27, 1927

In 1872 Woodhull became the first woman to run for president. As a member of the Equal Rights Party, she supported an eight-hour workday, women's right to vote, and new divorce laws.

Carol Moseley Braun

AUGUST 16, 1947–

Democrat Carol Moseley Braun was Illinois voters' pick for Senate in 1984. With the win she became the first African-American woman in the Senate.

Shirley Chisholm

NOVEMBER 30, 1924–JANUARY 1, 2005

Shirley Chisholm was a champion for women and minority rights. In 1972 she became the first African-American to seek the Democratic nomination for president. Although she didn't get their endorsement, she remained a bold force in politics.

Across the United States, women have crashed through nearly every door of every boys' club. Here are some of women's fabulous firsts.

Geraldine Ferraro

AUGUST 26, 1935–MARCH 26, 2011

The Democrats picked their first female vice presidential candidate in 1984. Geraldine Ferraro got an eight-minute standing ovation at the convention. The Democrats lost that election, but Ferraro remained a strong political force.

Sarah Palin

FEBRUARY 11, 1964–

In 2008 Alaska Governor Sarah Palin accepted the Republicans' nomination to be their first female candidate for vice president. Although they lost the election, Palin became a star in the Republican party.

Nancy Pelosi

MARCH 26, 1940–

In 2007 Nancy Pelosi became Speaker of the House of Representatives. A woman had never been elected to this powerful job before. Democrats applaud her forceful nature and fund-raising success.

INDIRA GHANDI

NOVEMBER 19, 1917–OCTOBER 31, 1984

INDIA'S CONTROVERSIAL LEADER KILLED

NEW DELHI, INDIA—Indira Ghandi, India's first female prime minister, was shot by her bodyguards today while walking in her garden.

Unknown to Ghandi, her bodyguards supported the political group Sikh Akali Dal. Ghandi had recently ordered the military to end a protest by the group, which wants to separate from India. Many members of the group died in the conflict. Ghandi knew the unpopular decision threatened her political career. Observers say she seemed to suspect the decision also threatened her life.

In a speech given hours before her murder, she said, "If I die today every drop of my blood will invigorate the nation."

International leaders opposed Ghandi's plans for nuclear weapons. They threatened to stop aid to India. But she believed her country needed a nuclear bomb because Pakistan could easily get one. Indians called her a hero for standing up to powerful countries.

"We would rather starve than sell our national honor," she said.

GIRLS RULE ANCIENT TIMES

In ancient times men were considered natural leaders. But women defied that narrow thinking and ruled their lands. They faced strong enemies and big obstacles. And they were clever, strong, and determined.

CLEOPATRA

69 BC—30 BC

Cleopatra's life story is pure Hollywood drama—love, betrayal, murder, and politics.

In her time the world belonged to the Roman Empire. The Romans swallowed independent countries and ruled them. Egypt's Queen Cleopatra was one of the few who were able to hold off the powerful Romans.

Cleopatra fought for Egypt's independence. But unlike other countries, she didn't go to war. Instead she used her charm, wit, and intelligence to capture the hearts of Roman leaders Julius Caesar and Marc Antony. And she lovingly convinced them to keep Rome out of Egypt, at least for awhile.

HATSHEPSUT

ABOUT 1508 BC–ABOUT 1458 BC

Fourteen centuries before Cleopatra, Hatshepsut ruled Egypt. When Hatshepsut's husband died, leaders agreed she would rule only until her stepson was old enough. But before the boy took the throne, Hatshepsut declared herself pharaoh. She led Egypt through 20 years of growth. She expanded trade and built good relationships with other countries.

But after her death, new leaders destroyed the temples and monuments honoring her. They tried to erase Hatshepsut from the history books to prevent another female from following her lead.

BOUDICCA

?–AD 62

Boudicca haunted Roman soldiers. Extremely tall, she had long, bushy red hair and a growling voice. Boudicca wore a black cape and a ring around her neck. In the dark she was a terrifying sight.

In AD 25, Rome was targeting Celtic tribes living in today's Great Britain. But Queen Boudicca wouldn't surrender her tribe's land. Instead, she united tribes and led an uprising.

She stunned Rome by winning a battle and killing thousands of Romans. Her followers burned ancient London, an area claimed by the Romans. Then Boudicca destroyed St. Albans, home to Romans and their local supporters.

Eventually Rome beat Boudicca's rebellion. But she had struck fear into the hearts of Roman soldiers. And she proved they could be beaten.

Russian President Mikahil Gorbachev called her "the Iron Lady." He meant to insult her.

BUT MARGARET THATCHER CONSIDERED IT A COMPLIMENT.

Thatcher was a serious, forceful, and persistent political leader. In 1979 she was elected the United Kingdom's first female prime minister. Her election was historic, but it was her policies that were truly radical.

The prime minister's actions made her a controversial figure. Thatcher believed citizens shouldn't rely so heavily on government help. She cut many programs for the poor. She let private businesses take over industries the government once controlled.

THATCHER ALSO STOOD STRONGLY AGAINST RUSSIA'S COMMUNIST GOVERNMENT.

World leaders feared a war was coming between Russia and the United States. U.S. President Ronald Reagan spent millions to build the world's mightiest military. Russia tried to match the United States dollar for dollar. Most world leaders stayed away from the conflict. Not Thatcher. She had forceful talks with President Gorbachev, pressing him to end his military build-up.

Many people believe Reagan was the superhero who brought Russia to its knees. Historians say they're wrong. Thatcher deserves the superhero label. Her persistent talks backed Gorbachev into a corner and kept the conflict from breaking into all-out war.

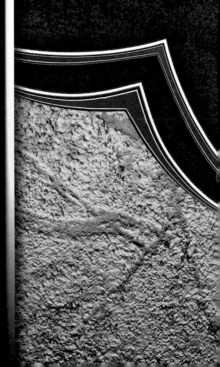

MARGARET
THATCHER

OCTOBER 13, 1925–APRIL 8, 2013

JUDGING BY THEIR CHARACTER

These extraordinary women made history not just because they were first, but because of their accomplishments and ability to bounce back from hard times.

Janet Reno

JULY 21, 1938–

Janet Reno was the first woman to serve as the U.S. Attorney General. In her role Reno advised the government in legal matters. She was forced to make one of her most debated decisions soon after she took the job in 1993.

A cult had built a compound in rural Texas. Led by David Koresh, cult members packed the place with weapons. Authorities confronted the group. Shots were fired. Several government agents and cult members died.

After a 51-day standoff, Reno ordered agents to use tear gas to flush out Koresh and his followers. A fire broke out, killing nearly 80 cult members. Nobody knew if the tear gas started the fire or if Koresh had started it. But Reno assumed personal responsibility for the order.

Although her decision stirred controversy, Reno won respect for taking responsibility and refusing to blame anyone else.

Margaret Chase Smith

DECEMBER 14, 1897–MAY 29, 1995

Senator Joseph McCarthy was the nation's biggest political bully in the 1950s. And Senator Margaret Smith wasn't about to back down to any bully.

Fear of communism swept through the United States after World War II. Communism is a system where the government controls the economy. McCarthy believed communist spies lurked in the nation. The powerful senator called hearings and accused people—many of whom were innocent—of plotting a communist uprising.

Some American leaders supported McCarthy's obsession with hunting communists. Others feared he'd target them if they disagreed. Not Senator Smith. She was the first U.S. Congressmember to publicly shame McCarthy and insist the attacks stop. In her famous speech, she said, "The American people are sick and tired of being afraid to speak their minds lest they be politically smeared as 'Communists' … Freedom of speech is not what it used to be in America. It has been so abused by some that it is not exercised by others."

Madeleine Albright

MAY 15, 1937–

As the first woman to serve as the U.S. Secretary of State, Madeleine Albright traveled across the globe to resolve international conflicts. One specific job involved negotiating peace between Israel's Jews and nearby Islamic countries.

This job wouldn't be easy. Albright's family was Jewish. Several of her relatives died in the Holocaust. Many Holocaust survivors had started new lives in Israel. She shared a common history with the people there.

But if she wanted peace, she could show no favoritism.

Albright met leaders in the Middle East. She condemned terrorism. She also pressed Israel's prime minister to sign peace treaties. She didn't favor either side, despite her personal heritage. Leaders worldwide respected her effort and praised her professionalism. Although the conflict brewed for years to come, President Barack Obama awarded Albright the 2012 Presidential Medal of Freedom for pursuing peace in the Middle East.

HILLARY CLINTON

OCTOBER 26, 1947–

"I'm in."

Two words. One historic moment.

In 2007 former first lady Hillary Clinton announced she was joining the presidential race and intended to be the first female president in U.S. history. "I'm in," she posted on her website. If anyone doubted her ambition, she added, "And I'm in to win."

Professionally, Clinton shattered many glass ceilings, the invisible barrier blocking women from important jobs. She'd been a lawyer, children's advocate, and political advisor. After her husband Bill Clinton's two terms as president, she leapt into politics. Clinton won a Senate seat and then aimed for the presidency.

But Senator Barack Obama wanted the job too.

Clinton and Obama went head-to-head, fighting for their party's nomination. The person who got the party's nod would be the Democratic candidate in the presidential election. The campaign was hard and historic. An African-American and a woman campaigned against each other. It was the first campaign of its kind in the United States. Whatever happened, the country would be forever changed.

Obama eventually won the nomination and later the election. But that did not take away from Clinton's achievements. She broke barriers for women in national politics. After the election, she thanked supporters, saying,

"Although we weren't able to shatter that highest, hardest glass ceiling this time, thanks to you, it's got about 18 million cracks in it."

President Obama recognized Clinton's abilities. He asked her to be his Secretary of State. This important role builds international relationships and resolves conflicts.
Again Clinton said, "I'm in!"

LEADING AROUND

Vigdís Finnbogadóttir

APRIL 15, 1930–

In 1980 artist Vigdís Finnbogadóttir narrowly won the presidential election. She became Iceland's first female president. As president her popularity soared.

Finnbogadóttir strengthened Iceland's identity and culture. She insisted on preserving its language. She also supported education.

Finnbogadóttir resigned after four terms. The country honored her with countless awards and created a new institute, the Vigdís Finnbogadóttir Institute of Foreign Language.

Joyce Banda APRIL 12, 1950–

Malawi, one of the world's poorest nations, is counting on new president Joyce Banda. Banda took control of the African nation in 2012 when President Bingu wa Mutharika died.

Malawi's people rely on aid from other countries. But countries had stopped sending help in protest of some of Mutharika's policies. Banda quickly reversed those policies, including giving the media back its independence. The aid returned.

Banda also rejected Mutharika's extravagant lifestyle. No more personal jets. No more luxury cars. The money, she argued, must be spent on her people.

THE WORLD

Sirimavo Bandaranaike

APRIL 17, 1916–OCTOBER 10, 2000

Bandaranaike's legacy stretches back to 1960 when she became the world's first female prime minister. When her husband was murdered, Bandaranaike took over his role as Sri Lanka's prime minister. As a socialist, she successfully continued her husband's quest to make the economy government controlled. While in power, she changed the country's name from Ceylon to Sri Lanka. A natural at foreign relations, Bandaranaike is credited with changing Sri Lanka from an isolated country into an international voice.

RULING FROM

The U.S. Supreme Court answers the nation's most important legal questions. It rules over every courtroom in the country. Elected officials—even presidents—must follow its decisions. The Supreme Court has nine members who serve lifetime terms. But until 1981 those nine members were always men.

How much do you know about the four women who have ruled from the Supreme Court's bench?

1. Who wrote a famous dissent, or written disagreement with a ruling? This dissent prompted Congress to pass a law making it easier for victims to sue for certain kinds of discrimination.

2. Which justice faced the most opposition to her appointment, with opponents saying she might let her heritage affect her ability to make fair decisions?

3. Who often held considerable power, being the tie-breaker vote when the court was split 4–4?

4. Which justice had never served as a judge until her appointment to the Supreme Court?

RETIRED JUSTICE
SANDRA DAY O'CONNOR

JUSTICE SONIA
SOTOMAYOR

THE BENCH

**JUSTICE RUTH
BADER GINSBERG**

**JUSTICE ELENA
KAGAN**

1. JUSTICE RUTH BADER GINSBERG
Served on the court from 1993–present

Her early legal experience came from the American Civil Liberties Union, which fights against discrimination. As a lawyer, she had a special interest in arguing cases involving discrimination against women.

2. JUSTICE SONIA SOTOMAYOR
Served on the court from 2009–present

Sotomayor's opponents worried she would relate to minority groups and favor their positions. Her appointment created debate about how religion, ethnicity, gender, and income might affect a justice's rulings.

3. JUSTICE SANDRA DAY O'CONNOR
Served on the court from 1981–2006

O'Connor was the first female justice to sit on the Supreme Court. During her appointment, the eight male justices were split. One group believed the Constitution changes over time. The other group believed the Constitution didn't change. O'Connor fell in the middle. Her tie-breaker decided important issues involving civil rights, privacy rights, and protecting the environment.

4. JUSTICE ELENA KAGAN
Served on the court from 2010–present

Although Kagan had never served as a judge, she has an impressive background. She was a professor, editor of a law magazine, and had advised the president. But without experience as a judge, lawmakers struggled to guess how she'd vote on major issues.

ANGELA MERKEL

JULY 17, 1954—

Her stomach growled. It was one of those weeks. Stores throughout East Germany had little food to sell. But that was a common problem in this country where the government owned everything.

But Angela Merkel didn't let her poor childhood keep her down. She excelled in math and science, earning her doctorate in physics. But as her knowledge grew, so did her frustration. She wanted a new government—one that would be run by the people.

In 1989 Merkel joined the growing democracy movement. East and West Germany had been divided by the Berlin Wall since World War II. West Germany had a democratic government. East Germany suffered under a controlling communist government. Merkel and many others wanted that wall to come down, reuniting East and West Germany. Later that year, she got her wish. The wall came down, and Angela started her life in politics.

She rose through the ranks quickly. Shortly after East and West Germany became one country, Merkel was appointed to the chancellor's cabinet. Soon she became the leader of her political party. And after just 16 years as a government leader, she was elected Germany's first female chancellor in 2005.

Living on a small budget became the center of Merkel's politics. She cut government jobs. She raised new money by taxing nuclear power plants. While other European countries choked on debt, Germany became the only country without major budget problems.

Leaders worldwide credit Merkel with Germany's rise to the strongest country in the European Union. Political watchers applaud her bright personality and careful handling of Germany's budget. The world is amazed at her determination to save her country.

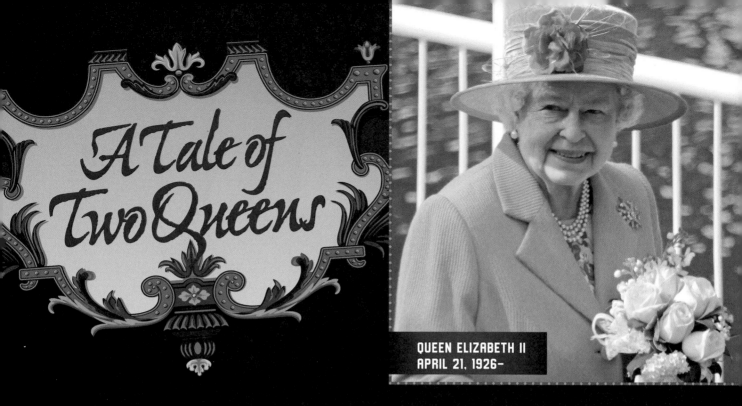

A Tale of Two Queens

QUEEN ELIZABETH II
APRIL 21, 1926–

Once upon a time, there lived two queens. Victoria was born in 1819, fifth in line for the royal throne. She never expected to be queen. But when her father and uncles died leaving no other heirs, the throne, and the responsibilities that went with it, all went to 19-year-old Victoria.

More than 100 years later, the story would almost repeat itself. Elizabeth was born in 1926, third in line for the royal throne. She never expected to be queen. But in 1936 her uncle, King Edward VIII, gave up the throne. He had no children, so Elizabeth's father became king. When he died, the throne, and the responsibilities that went with it, went to Elizabeth.

While the queens' stories are separated by time, they are linked by their similarities. As queens, both Elizabeth and Victoria danced at fancy balls, entertained other royalty, and traveled the country to meet their subjects.

They both also had their struggles. Both queens learned quickly that mistakes—big and small—circled the world in minutes. The smallest slip could bring shame to their royal courts.

Each queen ruled for more than 60 years. They represented their country with grace and dignity. And they helped their nation live happily ever after.

QUEEN VICTORIA
MAY 24, 1819–JANUARY 22, 1901

Timeline

1837 .... Victoria becomes queen of Great Britain.

1842 .... Victoria takes her first train ride to visit her people. She becomes the first monarch to recognize the importance of public appearances.

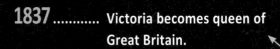

1860–1890 .. Victoria oversees an era during which day-to-day political power shifts from monarchs to elected officials.

1875 .... Victoria helps avoid a German-French war by influencing the German Emperor.

1877 .... Victoria expands British power by becoming Empress of India.

1900 .... Victoria continues to change royalty to be a champion of the people instead of political leaders. She visits soldiers, schools, and hospitals.

1940 .... At age 14, Elizabeth delivers her first radio address to calm children who had to be evacuated because of war.

1940s .... Princess Elizabeth serves her country during wartime by being trained as a military driver and mechanic.

1952 .... Elizabeth becomes queen of Great Britain.

1960s .... Elizabeth's glowing reputation helps forge a "new" Great Britain. British colonies gain independence, but most join a new Commonwealth. They remain independent but keep Elizabeth as their queen.

2012 .... Elizabeth celebrates 60 years as queen. The only other queen to celebrate the 60-year mark is Victoria, Elizabeth's great-great grandmother.

43

May 1948. In four days, Israeli leaders planned to announce their claim to Palestine as a home for Jews. Arabs called the Jewish plan an invasion, and they planned to fight it. War between the groups loomed. The world saw violence coming, but nobody knew how to prevent it.

Golda Meir intended to try. She wasn't a spy or an assassin. She was a woman who wanted to protect her people and their homeland.

"We have always said that in our war with the Arabs we had a secret weapon—no alternative."

Israel's prime minister had appointed Meir to be a member of Israel's new government. With the job came a dangerous mission. Disguised in a simple Muslim dress, she hid in a truck. Drivers smuggled her past groups of Arab soldiers, who waited for attack orders.

Once in Jordan, Meir walked confidently into a secret meeting with Jordan's King Abdullah. She boldly argued that Jordan should remain neutral and stay out of the coming war.

But King Abdullah refused, and soon the Middle East was at war.

Israel won the short war, but conflict continued. In 1969 Meir became Israel's prime minister, a rare feat in a region where politics belonged to men. She pledged to protect Israel, even if it meant another war.

Meir led the nation through another war and another victory. But that victory came at a price. More than 2,700 Israeli soldiers died in the war, a huge number in the small country. Citizens were devastated by the loss of life and took their anger out on their leader. After four years as prime minster, Meir resigned.

But over time the pain lessened. Citizens once again remembered what Meir had done for their country. Today Meir, the Mother of Israel, is an icon of independence—a legend who built the backbone of a determined nation.

WORLD-CLASS
First Ladies

Jacqueline "Jackie" Kennedy

JULY 28, 1929–MAY 19, 1994

wife of President John F. Kennedy

The world's most important people entertained at the White House. But Jackie Kennedy argued that it had not been taken care of and stood as a terrible reflection of the United States. Kennedy restored the White House, making it the country's prized national treasure.

She tracked down people who held White House relics, including antique furniture, rugs, china, and other valuable items. She convinced those people to donate the items back to the White House.

Caroline Harrison

OCTOBER 1, 1832–OCTOBER 25, 1892

wife of President Benjamin Harrison

Educated in art, music, and literature, Caroline Harrison was an accomplished artist. But citizens of the era didn't see public benefit from art. The government had no budget for it. Harrison supported artists and created an artistic legacy at the White House. She called her own press conference to seek a renovation budget for the White House—a tactic never before used by a first lady.

As an advocate for women's rights, she also pushed businesses and government to improve the lives of women. She even convinced John Hopkins Medical School to admit women.

Michelle Obama

JANUARY 19, 1964–

wife of President Barack Obama

Michelle Obama created Let's Move, a campaign to end childhood obesity. She brought children into the White House yard to plant a garden and showcase the importance of vegetables. Her goals are to create healthier school lunches and programs to lower the cost of healthy food for low-income families. She also plans to get the country exercising.

She's convinced teachers, doctors, nurses, and parents to join the cause and help spread the word in local communities.

"One of the lessons that I grew up with was to always stay true to yourself and never let what somebody else says distract you from your goals."

RULING THE WORLD OF BUSINESS

RUTH HANDLER

NOVEMBER 16, 1916–APRIL 27, 2002

I've been a doctor,
an astronaut, and a
presidential candidate.
I've even been a mermaid!
I own houses, bikes, campers,
convertibles, horses, jets, pools,
and so many clothes you'd need a
dream house to store them.

You know my name. Yeah, I'm Barbie.

In the 1950s my "mother," Ruth Handler, knew girls were tired of baby dolls. They craved a fashionable doll that actually looked like a young woman. After my stunning debut, girls begged parents to buy me. Now I have more than a billion Barbie sisters worldwide.

I've been around for a long time. I have watched some incredible women earn top jobs in business. My mother Ruth stuffed children's toy boxes.

Indra Nooyi and Irene Rosenfeld filled their families' kitchens. And Sheryl Sandberg transformed the social lives of kids and parents.

Ms. Nooyi runs Pepsi. She's the genius who realized that creating varieties of Pepsi would sell more than just one or two types. She also bet Pepsi would sell better globally if they tweaked the recipe and reflected local customs.

Ms. Rosenfeld made an unusual, bold move that got everyone talking and made profits zoom. Instead of buying up companies, which is the trend in business today, she split Kraft Foods into two companies. She also revived classics like Oreos.

Ms. Sandberg is a tech-and-business guru. She first did online sales for Google. Then she jumped to Facebook to do marketing and growth strategies. She helped Facebook grow from 70 million users to more than 750 million.

Even I'm impressed.

INDRA NOOYI
OCTOBER 28, 1955–

IRENE ROSENFELD
MAY 3, 1953–

SHERYL SANDBERG
AUGUST 28, 1969–

Madam C. J. Walker

DECEMBER 23, 1867–MAY 25, 1919

Sarah Breedlove was losing her hair. She'd tried several products that promised to help, but nothing worked. She began mixing, experimenting, and praying, all in the hope of creating a product that would work. What she developed was a recipe for success. All her African-American friends and family members wanted her secret solution.

Breedlove continued experimenting and created other products. She made skin care cream and an ointment that straightened thick coarse hair. Finally African-American women had beauty products designed specifically for them.

In the late 1800s, there weren't billboards or TV ads. Getting the word out about her new products proved to be a problem. But Breedlove had an idea—an idea that would become a popular sales strategy for more than a century. Now going by the name Madam C. J. Walker, she recruited women to sell the products door-to-door.

Her parents had been slaves. But with her revolutionary business idea, Madam C. J. Walker became the first African-American female millionaire in the United States.

"I had to make my own living and my own opportunity. But I made it! Don't sit down and wait for the opportunities to come. Get up and make them."

MARY KAY ASH

MAY 12, 1918–NOVEMBER 22, 2001

Mary Kay Ash's boss walked into her office and delivered the news. No raise or promotion for her. Again. He was giving it to her male coworker.

Ash fumed. Her male coworker made fewer sales than she did. But it was the 1950s, and discrimination like this was common. Ash wasn't going to put up with it anymore. She quit.

But then she had to find some other way to make money. Her former job involved demonstrating company products at home parties. She wondered if she could do the same kind of parties for beauty supplies.

Ash used her savings to launch a beauty-products company called Mary Kay. She built a marketing plan around a sales force of mostly stay-at-home moms who wanted extra money. They sold products at parties, earned a commission, and, if they met sales goals, won big prizes. Ash earned a million dollars in just two years.

Ash's business model was very similar to the one Madam C. J. Walker created. No one knows for sure if Ash learned from Walker's business. But we do know that both women made millions of dollars in times when men ruled the business world.

Margaret Chan

Hong Kong, 1997. Eighteen people hospitalized. Six dead. Hundreds more infected. No vaccines, no treatments. Lab tests showed a new, deadly flu virus ... and it was spreading from chickens to humans.

The virus couldn't have happened in a worse place. Chickens packed markets and roamed in millions of backyards in Hong Kong—one of the most crowded places in the world. People were in constant contact with the birds. If something wasn't done, the consequences could be catastrophic.

The mystery virus required a medical detective. Dr. Margaret Chan, the country's health chief, took charge of the case. Working with scientists across the globe, she investigated the options.

But the clock ticked away. Flu viruses spread easily.

Within days the virus could spread worldwide. Millions of people could get sick and even die.

As panic spread Chan had to make a decision. She made a bold choice. She ordered that every chicken and duck in the country be killed—1.5 million in all. The world watched and wondered whether the controversial plan would end the outbreak.

IT DID.

Experts praised Chan's bold action. The World Health Organization, which monitors deadly diseases across the globe, asked her to lead its work.

Chan now advises countries about ways to stop deadly diseases. She is a warrior of public health, fighting for bigger budgets, more research, and worldwide preparation to fight new illnesses.

"There is a cost for investing in preparedness, but a much bigger cost for not investing."

CLARA BARTON

DECEMBER 25, 1821–APRIL 12, 1912

American soldiers were dying in hospitals and on battlefields. Doctors didn't have medicine and supplies for the hundreds of injured soldiers. But they had Clara Barton.

The United States was fighting the bloody Civil War in the 1860s. Barton marched onto battlefields as a nurse for northern troops. Her bravery and care earned her the nickname "angel of the battlefield."

After the war Barton learned about a relief organization in Europe. Called the International Red Cross, the group helped people recover from disasters. Their work impressed Barton and moved her to call for an American branch.

The American Red Cross opened in 1881 with Barton as president. The organization grew under her leadership. Barton served for five years and never took any pay.

The angel of the battlefield became the angel in disaster's wake.

MARTHA STEWART

AUGUST 3, 1941–

Martha Stewart turned homemaking into big business.

In the late 1970s, Stewart quit her job as a stockbroker. She launched a catering business from her basement. Soon her menus and unique presentations made her a sought-after caterer. Her business was worth $1 million after just 10 years.

Stewart expanded her business with her first book, *Martha Stewart's Entertaining*. The book was a best-seller. Then career achievements began to fall like dominoes.

HOLIDAY SPECIALS ON TV

MORE BOOKS

A MAGAZINE

A TV SHOW

SOON STEWART'S NAME APPEARED ON PRODUCTS
SUCH AS SHEETS, TOWELS, AND DECORATIONS.

If fans planned to decorate a bathroom or host a
dinner party, they turned to Stewart for advice.
And they could find her advice everywhere.

MARTHA STEWART BECAME THE
RICHEST HOMEMAKER OF ALL TIME.

JOAN GANZ COONEY

NOVEMBER 30, 1929–

For nearly 50 years, the colorful friends of *Sesame Street* have taught kids to read, count, and be good friends. But it wasn't the puppets that built a new world in children's entertainment. That was Joan Ganz Cooney.

JOAN COONEY'S APARTMENT

In 1966 Cooney wondered if children's TV shows could be entertaining and educational.

DOWN THE STREET

Cooney leads the development of other kids' shows, including *The Electric Company*.

SESAME STREET BANK

Cooney gets start-up money for programming from the Carnegie and Ford foundations.

SESAME STREET AUDITORIUM

Cooney and her team win their first Emmy Award in 1970 for Outstanding Achievement in Children's Programming.

SESAME STREET SCHOOL

Cooney gets help from educators to develop guidelines for the show to make sure it truly advances kids' learning.

JIM HENSON'S APARTMENT

Cooney's show, *Sesame Street*, debuts in 1969, featuring famous puppeteer Jim Henson.

You can call Katie Couric professional. Call her smart, creative, tough. Just do not call her perky.

"If I hear the word 'perky' again, I'll puke."

After 30 successful years in the news business, Couric is known for her powerful reporting. But she's just as well known for her positive personality. In 2006 Couric became the first woman to lead an evening news broadcast without a male cohost. But she'd been a superstar long before her first newscast on CBS.

Producers of a struggling morning program called *Today* needed an injection of sparkle to boost ratings. They hired Couric.

And she sparkled. With her warm smile, energetic personality, and sense of humor, *Today* quickly became the number one morning show.

But Couric was no pushover. She flipped from warm to tough for serious interviews.

She also broke the mold for reporting stories. When her husband died from colon cancer, she made cancer prevention a personal news story. Couric allowed her colon cancer test, a very private procedure, to be broadcast on national television.

Her skills and popularity got her the largest paycheck in broadcast news—a four-year $65 million contract. She's proven that a journalist can be informative, fun, inspiring … and perky.

KATIE COURIC

JANUARY 7, 1957–

THE LIFE AND TIMES OF
ALICE WALKER

FEBRUARY. 9, 1944–

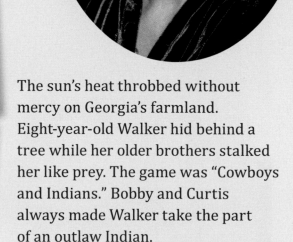

Chapter 1:

Humble Beginnings:

Alice Malsenior Walker is born the last of eight children in a poor family of African-American sharecroppers.

Chapter 2:

Marriage and Family:

Walker, husband Mel, and daughter Rebecca fight for civil rights in the 1960s.

Chapter 3:

The Young Writer:

Walker writes poetry and stories about African-American women coping in a sexist, racist society.

Chapter 4:

Award-winning novel:

The Color Purple, Walker's third novel, hits the best-seller list and becomes a movie starring Oprah Winfrey.

Chapter 5:

Always an Activist:

Walker is recognized for her civil rights work, not just because of her activism, but because of her award-winning novels that tackle social issues.

The sun's heat throbbed without mercy on Georgia's farmland. Eight-year-old Walker hid behind a tree while her older brothers stalked her like prey. The game was "Cowboys and Indians." Bobby and Curtis always made Walker take the part of an outlaw Indian.

Walker peeked around the tree just as Curtis raised his BB gun and fired. The pellet burned through the air and sliced into Walker's right eye. An innocent child's game left her unable to see from her right eye.

The scarring embarrassed her. She turned into a shy girl who spent her time with books instead of friends. But the horrible injury influenced her literature career by making her an avid reader. She learned about great writing, and she learned to develop her own voice.

Short Stories:
OTHER LEADERS IN LITERATURE

Ida Tarbell
NOVEMBER 5, 1857–JANUARY 6, 1944

Ida Tarbell was a writer and editor. She did careful research and a series of articles about the oil industry. This new reporting—investigative journalism—changed newspapers and magazines. Journalists took on a new role of investigator and exposed corruption. Her 19-part series, "The History of the Standard Oil Company," was listed number five among the top 100 works of 20th-century American journalism.

Toni Morrison
FEBRUARY 18, 1931–

Toni Morrison is a well-known African-American writer whose books deal with powerful topics. In 1993 she became the first African-American woman to win the Nobel Prize for literature.

Joanne "J. K." Rowling
JULY 31, 1965–

Rowling's rags-to-riches story is almost as famous as her books. Despite poverty, she refused to give up her dream of writing novels. She struck gold when *Harry Potter and the Sorcerer's Stone* was finally published. The seven-book Harry Potter series is among the most popular works of all time.

OPRAH

Winfrey

JANUARY 29, 1954-

When Oprah speaks the whole world listens.

Oprah Winfrey is one of the most powerful people in the world. She didn't build her empire with hostile takeovers, though. She built her reputation by building trust. For years Winfrey told her TV audience about her mistakes, problems, and deepest secrets. Winfrey created a relationship with viewers that turned her into their televised best friend.

Because they loved and trusted her, Winfrey could move people to do amazing things.

In 1996 Winfrey started a book club. That club soon proved the power this woman had. Her first book club choice was Jacquelyn Mitchard's *The Deep End of the Ocean*. Within weeks the book became a best-seller. In fact, every one of Winfrey's book club selections sold more than 1 million copies.

Media experts called it the "Oprah Effect." Anything she recommended—from books to perfumes to pillows—turned into a best-seller.

Her fame brought her fortune. *Forbes* magazine called Winfrey the richest African-American of the 20th century. In 2011 Winfrey ended her long-running program, *The Oprah Winfrey Show*. She moved to her own network. The transition was rocky, but in 2013 she interviewed cyclist Lance Armstrong. Millions of viewers tuned in, proving that the world is still listening to their friend Oprah.

Throughout history women have proven they have the power, courage, and strength to lead. From launching businesses to improving the lives of others, women have kicked open the doors of change.

Some people think it's easier to accept the world's problems than change them. But leaders act on their beliefs. Female leaders have leapt over barriers and paved history with stories of inspiration.

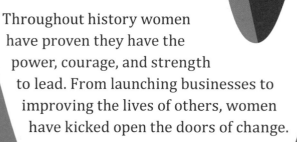

THEIR STORIES LEAVE NO DOUBT—GIRLS RULE!

MANY OF THESE WOMEN LED OVER SEVERAL DECADES.
THEIR PLACEMENT ON THE TIMELINE REFLECTS THE
DECADE IN WHICH THEY TRULY MADE HISTORY.

Ancient Times
Boudicca
Cleopatra
Hatshepsut

1870s
Queen Victoria
Victoria Woodhull

1880s
Caroline Harrison
Clara Barton

1900s
Ida Tarbell
Madam C. J. Walker

1910s
Jane Addams
Rosa Luxemburg

1920s
Mary McLeod Bethune

1930s
Eleanor Roosevelt

1940s
Eva Perón

1950s
Margaret Chase Smith
Ruth Handler

1960s
Dolores Huerta
Jacqueline Kennedy
Mary Kay Ash
Queen Elizabeth II
Sirimavo Bandaranaike

1970s
Golda Meir
Indira Ghandi
Joan Ganz Cooney
Shirley Chisholm

1980s
Alice Walker
Benazir Bhutto
Carol Moseley Braun
Corazon Aquino
Geraldine Ferraro
Margaret Thatcher
Sandra Day O'Connor
Vigdís Finnbogadóttir
Wilma Mankiller
Winnie Mandela

1990s
Aung San Suu Kyi
Janet Reno
Madeleine Albright
Margaret Chan
Martha Stewart
Oprah Winfrey
Ruth Bader Ginsberg
Toni Morrison

2000s
Angela Merkel
Hillary Clinton
J. K. Rowling
Katie Couric
Nancy Pelosi
Queen Rania
Sarah Palin
Sonia Sotomayor
Indra Nooyi
Marissa Mayer

2010s
Elena Kagan
Irene Rosenfeld
Joyce Banda
Michelle Obama
Sheryl Sandberg

INDEX

READ MORE

Ball, Heather. *Women Leaders Who Changed the World.* Great Women of Achievement. New York: Rosen Central, 2012.

McCann, Michelle Roehm and Amelie Welden. *Girls Who Rocked the World: Heroines from Joan of Arc to Mother Teresa.* New York: Aladdin, 2012.

Schwartz, Heather E. *Girls Rebel!: Amazing Tales of Women Who Broke the Mold.* Girls Rock. North Mankato, Minn.: Capstone Press, 2014.

INTERNET SITES

FactHound offers a safe, fun way to find Internet sites related to this book. All of the sites on FactHound have been researched by our staff.

Here's all you do:

Visit *www.facthound.com*

Type in this code: 9781476502359